# About Mastering Basic Skills—"Real-Life" Math Word Problems:

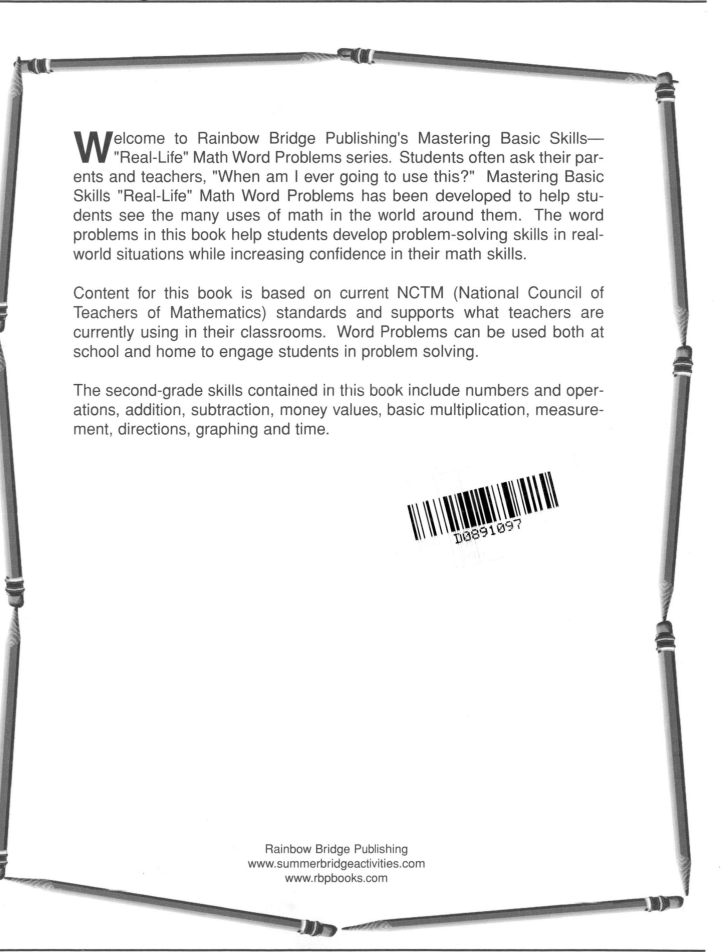

**W**elcome to Rainbow Bridge Publishing's Mastering Basic Skills—"Real-Life" Math Word Problems series. Students often ask their parents and teachers, "When am I ever going to use this?" Mastering Basic Skills "Real-Life" Math Word Problems has been developed to help students see the many uses of math in the world around them. The word problems in this book help students develop problem-solving skills in real-world situations while increasing confidence in their math skills.

Content for this book is based on current NCTM (National Council of Teachers of Mathematics) standards and supports what teachers are currently using in their classrooms. Word Problems can be used both at school and home to engage students in problem solving.

The second-grade skills contained in this book include numbers and operations, addition, subtraction, money values, basic multiplication, measurement, directions, graphing and time.

D0891097

Rainbow Bridge Publishing
www.summerbridgeactivities.com
www.rbpbooks.com

# Table of Contents

# Planning a Field Trip to the Zoo

Name _____  Date _____

◇ **Start Here!**

Your class is planning a field trip to the zoo on March 10.  Use the calendar to answer the questions below.

## March

| Sunday | Monday | Tuesday | Wednesday | Thursday | Friday | Saturday |
|---|---|---|---|---|---|---|
|  |  | 1 | 2 | 3 | 4 | 5 |
| 6 | 7 | 8 | 9 | 10 <br> Field trip! | 11 | 12 |
| 13 | 14 | 15 | 16 | 17 | 18 | 19 |
| 20 | 21 | 22 | 23 | 24 | 25 | 26 |
| 27 | 28 | 29 | 30 | 31 |  |  |

1 The class field trip to the zoo is on March 10th.  Draw an animal picture on that day.

2 What day of the week is March 10th? _____

3 How many days must you wait before you go to the zoo if today is March 1?

_____

4 How many Saturdays are there before the field trip? _____

5 Draw a clover on March 17th for St. Patrick's Day.

6 How many days are there between the zoo trip and St. Patrick's Day? _____

Name _____     Date _____

## ◇ Start Here!

Read the clues below. Draw each bird in its correct square. Write its ordinal number.

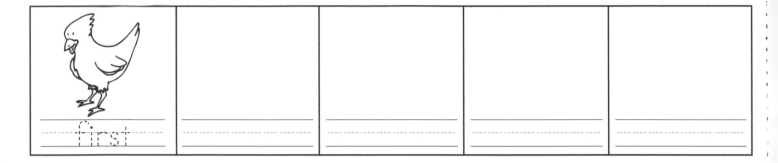

| | | | | |
|---|---|---|---|---|
|  *first* | | | | |

| | | Picture Bank | Word Bank |
|---|---|---|---|
|  **1** | The cardinal is first in line. |  | first |
|  **2** | Beside the cardinal is the toucan. | | second |
|  **3** | The duck is fourth in line. |  | third |
|  **4** | The hummingbird is in front of the duck. |  | fourth |
| **5** | The turkey is last in line. | | fifth |

Draw a picture.

| Who came in second? | Who came in fourth? |
|---|---|
| | |

# The Race in the Bear Den

Name _____    Date _____

## ◇ Start Here!

Read the clues below. Draw each bear in its correct square. Write its ordinal number.

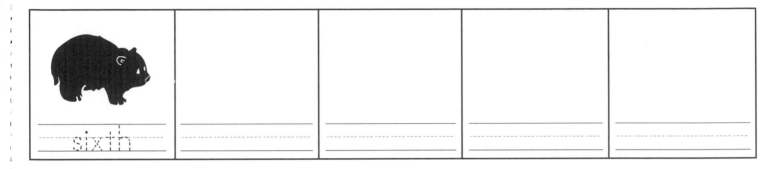

sixth

|  |  | Picture Bank | Word Bank |
|---|---|---|---|

 **1**  The black bear is sixth in line.

 **2**  The teddy bear is last in line.

 **3**  In front of him is the polar bear.

 **4**  The koala bear is behind the black bear.

 **5**  The panda bear is eighth.

Picture Bank | Word Bank

 sixth

 seventh

 eighth

 ninth

 tenth

Draw a picture.

| Who is in seventh place? | Who is in ninth place? |
|---|---|
|  |  |

**MBS—Math Word Problems Grade 2**

# Animal Clues

Name _____  Date _____

### ◇ Start Here!
Draw the animals in the squares to find the answers.

**1** The duck is first. The frog is between the tadpole and the duck. The fish is next to the tadpole. Where is the snake? _____

| | | | | |
|---|---|---|---|---|
| (duck) | (frog) | (tadpole) | (fish) | (snake) |

**2** The frog is first. The tadpole is between the frog and the snake. The fish is fourth. Where is the duck? _____

| | | | | |
|---|---|---|---|---|
| | | | | |

**3** The duck is last. The tadpole is between the duck and the snake. The frog is second. Where is the fish? _____

| | | | | |
|---|---|---|---|---|
| | | | | |

**4** The frog is second. The snake is last. The fish is between the duck and the snake. Where is the tadpole? _____

| | | | | |
|---|---|---|---|---|
| | | | | |

- - - - - - - - - - - - - - - - - - - - - - - - - - - - - - - - - - - - - - - - - -

|  |  |  |  |  |
|---|---|---|---|---|
| frog | duck | fish | tadpole | snake |

# Mammal Table

Name _____  Date _____

## ◇Start Here!

Use the tally marks to fill in the mammal table. Then answer the questions.

| | 🦛 | 🐘 | 🐱 |
|---|---|---|---|
| Jeff saw  II hippos  IIII elephants  III tigers | 2 | 4 | 3 |
| Brooke saw  I hippo  II elephants  III tigers | | | |
| Abbie saw  III hippos  IIII elephants  I tiger | | | |
| Matt saw  I hippo  III elephants  II tigers | | | |
| TOTAL | | | |

1. Who saw the most hippos? _____

2. Who saw the least elephants? _____

3. How many tigers were seen in all? _____

4. How many more elephants were seen than hippos? _____

Name _____  Date _____

**◇Start Here!**

Use the number sentences to solve the problem.  Draw in the animals.

---

**1**   There were 10 hippos at the zoo.

5 more were born.

How many hippos were there?

    10    +    5    = ___**15**___ hippos

---

**2**   There were 9 monkeys at the zoo.

7 more came.

How many monkeys are there at the zoo?

    9    +    7    = _____ monkeys

---

**3**   There are 8 mother kangaroos at the zoo.

Each has a baby in its pouch.

How many kangaroos are there altogether?

    8    +    8    = _____ kangaroos

---

**4**   There were 4 lions at the zoo.

7 more were born.

How many lions are at the zoo now?

    4    +    7    = _____ lions

---

| Picture Bank |  |  |  |  |
|---|---|---|---|---|
| | hippo | monkey | kangaroo | lion |

# What Bugs Me?

Name _____     Date _____

## ◇ Start Here!

Read each problem. Draw a picture. Write a number sentence with the answer.

**①** 5 bees flew to the hive from the roses.
9 more bees came from the dandelions.
How many bees were there altogether?

**5 + 9 = 14**    bees

**②** 4 snails crawled in the grass.
8 more came out of the weeds.
How many were there in all?

snails

**③** 6 flies fell into the spider's web.
Right away 9 more fell into the web.
How many flies fell into the web?

flies

**④** 2 ladybugs were on a leaf.
6 more landed on the leaf.
Then 7 more came.
How many ladybugs were on the leaf?

ladybugs

| Picture Bank | | | | |
|---|---|---|---|---|
|  spider |  ladybug |  fly |  snail | bee |

Name _____     Date _____

## ◇ Start Here!

Solve the number sentence.  Draw a picture to help you.

---

**1**  The deer flipped his tail at 14 flies.  6 of them flew away.  How many are left?

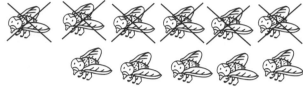

14   -   6   =   **8**   deer flies

---

**2** You find 13 beetles on a flower.  A bird eats 7 of them.  How many are left?

13   -   7   =  _____  beetles

---

**3** While camping, 15 dragonflies land on your fishing pole.  You brush 9 dragonflies off.  How many are still on your pole?

15   -   9   =  _____  dragonflies

---

**4** There were 17 cocoons.  10 of them turned into butterflies.  How many are still cocoons?

17   -   10   =  _____  cocoons

---

| Picture Bank |  |  |  |  |  |  |
|---|---|---|---|---|---|---|
| | beetle | cocoon | dragonfly | bird | butterfly | fly |

---

Name _____      Date _____

## ◇ Start Here!

Write the number sentence on the line.

---

**1** The tarantula caught 11 grasshoppers for breakfast and 6 flies for lunch. How many munchies did he catch that day?

$$11 + 6 = 17$$

**2** The tarantula has 7 potato beetles in his burrow. 7 more walked in. How many munchies does he have?

_____

---

**3** There were 18 flies flying past the burrow. 5 flies got caught. How many flies did not get caught? _____

---

**4** There are 14 dragonflies in the burrow with the tarantula. How many more dragonflies are there than tarantulas?

_____

**5** If the tarantula catches 3 silverfish a day for 4 days, how many silverfish will he have altogether?

_____

---

**6** There are 13 termites caught in the tarantula's burrow, but 2 of them get away. How many are still caught? _____

---

Write a munchy sentence of your own.

_____

_____

_____

_____

# Feeding the Animals

Name _____     Date _____

┌─────────────────────────────────────────────────────┐
│ ◇ **Start Here!**                                    │
│ Answer the questions.                                │
└─────────────────────────────────────────────────────┘

Lizard:
Eats 2 flies
each day.

Frog:
Eats 3
ladybugs
a day.

Turtle:
Eats 1 fish
each day.

Monkey:
Eats 6
bananas a day.

Use the information above to solve the problems.

| | |
|---|---|
| **1** Three lizards each eat flies. How many flies will they eat?<br><br>**2 + 2 + 2 = 6** | **2** A frog eats ladybugs for 2 days. How many ladybugs will the frog eat? |
| **3** Six turtles are eating fish today. How many fish will they eat together? | **4** Two monkeys eat bananas today. How many bananas did they eat? |

Name _____     Date _____

## ◇ Start Here!

Read each problem. Draw a picture to help you solve the problem.

---

**1** There is one ostrich and one toucan. How many legs?

$$2 + 2 = 4$$
_____

**2** There are three beetles. How many legs?

_____

---

**3** There are two elephants and one mouse. How many legs?

_____

**4** There is one beetle, one spider and one elephant. How many legs?

_____

---

**5** There are two toucans and two spiders. Which group has the most legs?

_____

**6** A snake crawls along the sand. How many legs?

_____

---

| Picture Bank | | | | | |
|---|---|---|---|---|---|
|  ostrich |  toucan |  elephant |  spider |  beetle | mouse |

Name _____    Date _____

## ◇ Start Here!

Follow the tree limbs to see which bird you will see.
Write the birds you visit on the way.

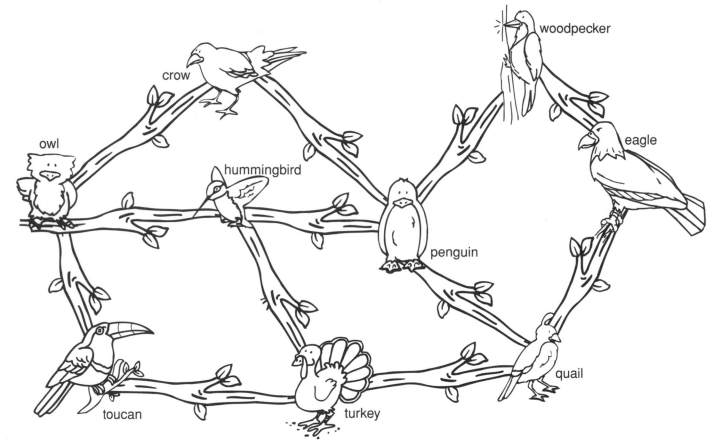

START

| toucan | ➡ | turkey | ➡ | quail | ➡ | eagle | END |
| owl | ➡ | | ➡ | | ➡ | woodpecker |
| eagle | ➡ | | ➡ | | ➡ | hummingbird |
| crow | ➡ | | ➡ | | ➡ | turkey |

Write your own.

_____ ➡ _____ ➡ _____ ➡ _____

Name _____     Date _____

**Start Here!**

Use arrows to mark the direction you must go to get from place to place in the zoo.

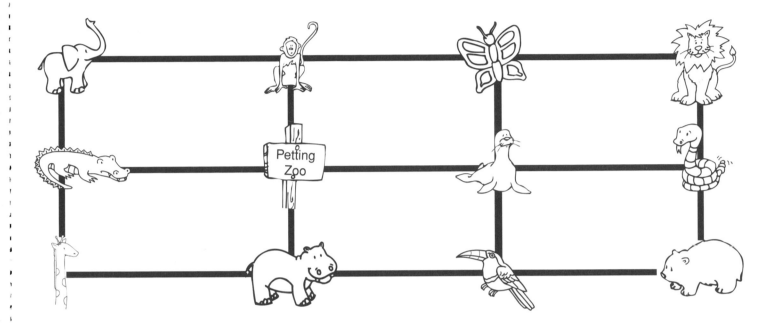

1. How do you get from the lions to the hippos?

   lions ⬇  ⬅  ⬅  ⬇  hippos

2. How do you get from the monkeys to the toucan?

   monkeys ____  ____  ____  toucan

3. How do you get from the  giraffes to the the lions?

   giraffes ____  ____  ____  ____  ____  lions

4. How do you get from the elephants to the bears?

   elephants ____  ____  ____  ____  ____  bears

# What Temperature Is Best?

Name _____     Date _____

◇ **Start Here!**

Write the temperature. Write warm or cold.

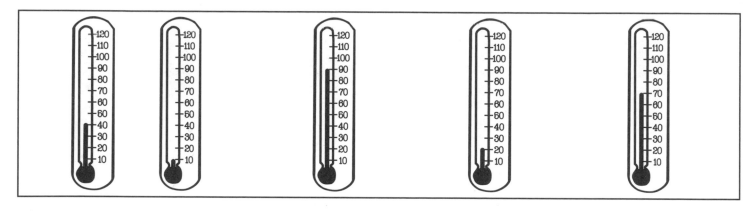

**1**  40°F     _____°F     _____°F     _____°F     _____°F

**2**  cold     _____     _____     _____     _____

Circle the temperature that is the better estimate for the animals.

**3**  Lizard on a rock.
    90°F    50°F

Squirrels gathering nuts.
    89°F    44°F

**4**  Frogs on a pond.
    22°F    60°F

Penguins on an iceberg.
    20°F    52°F

Name _____      Date _____

◇ **Start Here!**

Complete the graph. Answer the questions.

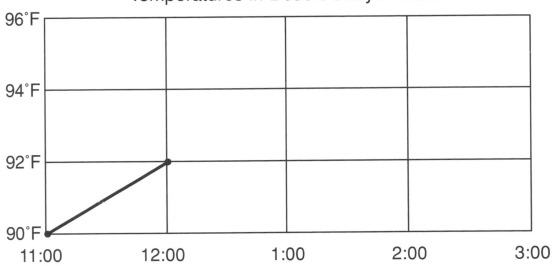

Temperatures in Desert Canyon Land

Read the sentences and complete the graph.

At 1:00 it was 96°F.
At 2:00 it was 94°F.
At 3:00 it was 94°F.

Use the line graph to help you solve the following questions.

1. What was the temperature at 12:00? _____ **92°** _____

2. What time was the hottest? _____

3. Was it warmer at 11:00 or 2:00? _____

4. Was it cooler at 12:00 or 3:00? _____

Name _____     Date _____

## ◇Start Here!

Read the sentences and answer the questions.

An elephant's tail is
is scruffy and thin.

A monkey's tail
is long and curled.

A bear's tail is
short and stubby.

A squirrel's tail is
thick and fluffy.

A lizard can lose
his tail and grow
another.

1  Who has the longest tail? _____

2  Who has the shortest tail? _____

3  Who has the thickest tail? _____

4  Who has the thinnest tail? _____

5  Who can lose his tail and grow another? _____

Name _____     Date _____

## ◇ Start Here!

Answer the questions.

8 lbs.

19 lbs.

50 lbs.

16 lbs.

30 lbs.

**1** Which baby weighs the least? _____

**2** Which baby weighs the most? _____

**3** How many more pounds does the baby elephant weigh than the baby hippo? _____

**4** Which baby weighs more than any two other babies added together? _____

**5** How much less does the baby monkey weigh than the baby bear? _____

# Favorite Zoo Mammals

Name _____   Date _____

### ◇ Start Here!

Look at the graph and complete the information below.

**①** _____**21**_____ children wrote down their choice.

**②** _____ children like hippos.

**③** More children like _____ than elephants.

**④** Fewer children like _____ than lions.

**⑤** The same number of children like elephants as _____.

**⑥** There are _____ more children who like monkeys better than lions.

**⑦** Which zoo animal was most liked by the students? _____

### Students' Favorite Zoo Animals

5 Lions

9 Monkeys

5 Elephants

2 Hippos

Make your own circle graph of the animals students in your class like.

| Animals | | | | |
|---|---|---|---|---|
| Tally marks | | | | |

Write your own question.

# Bird Speed  Graph

Name _____  Date _____

## ◇ Start Here!
Use the table to solve.  Write the number sentence to show your work.

1. How much faster is the eagle than the duck?

   **100 – 70 = 30**

2. Which bird flies the fastest?

   _____

3. Which bird flies the slowest?

   _____

4. If the sea gull's speed was doubled, how fast would it be flying?

   _____

5. What is the difference between the hummingbird's speed and the pigeon's speed?

   _____

| Birds | Speed per Hour |
|-------|----------------|
| hummingbird | 120 |
| eagle | 100 |
| hawk | 90 |
| duck | 70 |
| pigeon | 60 |
| sea gull | 50 |

6. Put the flight speed in order from slowest to fastest.

   ____  ____  ____  ____  ____  ____

7. Put the flight speed in order from fastest to slowest.

   ____  ____  ____  ____  ____  ____

# Lunch at the Zoo

Name _____     Date _____

◇ **Start Here!**

Answer the questions.

---

**MENU**

**Sandwiches**

| | | | |
|---|---|---|---|
| Cheese | $1.00 | Chicken | $1.75 |
| Ham | $1.25 | Hamburger | $1.50 |

**Drinks**

| | | | |
|---|---|---|---|
| Milk | .50¢ | Juice | .60¢ |
| Soda | .40¢ | Milk Shake | .75¢ |

**Money Bank**

---

1. You have $2.00. What will you order? How much change will you have left? Show us below.

2. Your friend has $3.00. What will he order? How much change will he have left? Show us below.

3. What is the difference between the cost your lunch and your friend's? Write a number sentence.

_____

4. What is the total cost of both meals? Write a number sentence.

_____

Name _____  Date _____

## ◇Start Here!

Answer the questions.

elephant 14¢

hippo 15¢

kangaroo 16¢

tiger 2¢

panda bear 10¢

bat 13¢

koala 17¢

**1** You have $1.00 to spend on stickers.

Fill out the order form to show the stickers you want to buy.

| Name of Sticker | How Many | Cost per One | Total Cost |
| --- | --- | --- | --- |
|  |  |  |  |
|  |  |  |  |
|  |  |  |  |
|  |  |  |  |
|  |  |  |  |
|  |  |  |  |
|  |  |  |  |

Total Cost for All the Stickers _____

**2** Which sticker costs the most? _____

**3** Which sticker costs the least? _____

**4** Which sticker is your favorite? _____

Name _____  Date _____

◇ **Start Here!**

Finish the story about the tigers. Write the number sentence after each part of the story.

**1**   10 tigers lay in the grass. 3 went to the water to get a drink. Then there

were ____**7**____ tigers left in the grass.    **10 - 3 = 7**

**2**   5 more tigers came in from hunting. Now there are _____ tigers in the

grass. _____

**3**   2 tigers left to find shade under a tree. How many tigers are still in the grass?

_____

**4**   4 tigers came back from sleeping. Finally there are _____ tigers in the

grass. _____

Choose your favorite animal and write your own numerical story.

# Kangaroos on the Loose!

Name _____     Date _____

### ◇ Start Here!

Count by fives.

backward   **5   10   15   20   25   30   35   40   45   50**   forward

You are following the kangaroo.  Write the number that tells where you land.

**1** Start at 5.
Hop forward 2 times.
Where will you end up?

**15**

**2** Start at 20.
Hop forward 4 times.
Where will you land?

_____

**3** Start at 35.
Jump forward 3 times.
What number are you on now?

_____

**4** Start at 40.
Jump backward 4 times.
Where do you land?

_____

**5** Start at 35.
Hop backward 1 time.
What number did you stop on?

_____

**6** Write your own.

Start at _____.
You want to get to _____.
How many hops did it take?

_____

Name _____          Date _____

◇**Start Here!**

You have 1 hour. Which animals will you be able to see?

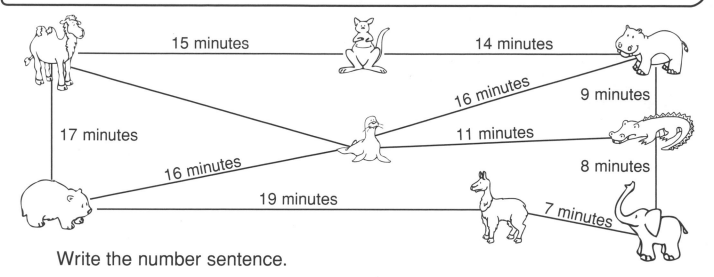

Write the number sentence.

**1**  How many minutes will it take you to get from the camels to

the llamas? _____ **17 + 19 = 36** _____

**2**  From the hippos will it take longer to get to the bears or camels? _____

Show why. _____

**3**  If you start by seeing the seals and then visit the hippos and kangaroos, how

many minutes will it take you? _____

**4**  Use your hour to see the zoo. Show which animals you can see in 60 minutes.

_____ to _____ takes _____ minutes

_____ to _____ takes _____ minutes

_____ to _____ takes _____ minutes

Total minutes _____

# Shows at the Zoo

**Time**

Name _____   Date _____

## ◇ Start Here!

Look at the times for the zoo shows.  Answer the questions.

---

**Elephant Ride**
1 hour
9:00     10:00
11:00     12:00

**Tropical Gardens**
15 minutes
9:15     10:15

**World of Flight Bird Arena**
1 hour
9:00     10:00
11:00     12:00

**Water Show**
30 minutes
11:00

**Petting Zoo**
15 minutes
10:30     11:30

**Zoofari Express Train**
45 minutes
9:30     10:30
11:30     12:30

---

Circle Your Answer

**1**   If you go on the Elephant Ride at 9:00, will you be able to go       yes       no
to the Tropical Garden right after and make the 10:15 show?

**2**   If you go on the Zoofari Express Train at 10:30, will you be       yes       no
able to make it to the Water Show at 11:00?

**3**   If you go to the Petting Zoo at 11:30, will you be able to get       yes       no
to the Bird Arena to see the show by 12:00?

Find a classmate.
Write down the name of the activity and the time you would like to do together.

_____

Name _____

Date _____

## ◇ Start Here!

Read and answer the questions.

**1** I am a number between
14 and 22.
I am 4 more than 16
What number am I?__**20**__

**2** I am an odd number between
20 and 30.
I am 9 more than 12.
What number am I?_____

**3** I am a number between
10 and 20.
I am 6 more than 14 - 6
What number am I?_____

**4** I am an odd number between
7 and 13.
I am 15 less than 26
What number am I?_____

**5** I am an odd number between
9 and 15.
I am not the sum of 6 + 5.
What number am I?_____

**6** Write one of your own.

_____

_____

# Stripes and Spots

Name _____  Date _____

**◇ Start Here!**
Read the questions. Solve the problems.

**1** There are 3 zebras that each have 25 stripes. How many stripes are there altogether?

| | 2 | 5 |
|---|---|---|
| | 2 | 5 |
| + | 2 | 5 |

| 7 | 5 |
|---|---|

**2** 3 tigers each have 22 stripes on them. How many stripes are on the tigers altogether?

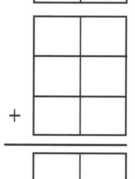

**3** If there are 2 snakes that have 15 white stripes, how many stripes will you have altogether?

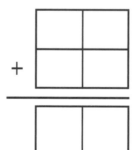

**4** A raccoon's tail has 4 black and 4 white stripes. If there are 4 raccoons, how many black stripes do they have?

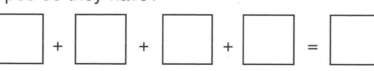

☐ + ☐ + ☐ + ☐ = ☐

www.rbpbooks.com  reproducible  **MBS—Math Word Problems Grade 2**

# How Many Animal Parts?

Name _____  Date _____

### ◇ Start Here!
Write a multiplication number sentence.

1. How many eyes?

    ___5___ x ___2___ = ___10___

2. How many tails?

    _____ x _____ = _____

3. How many ears?

    _____ x _____ = _____

4. How many legs?

    _____ x _____ = _____

5. How many wings?

    _____ x _____ = _____

6. How many paws?

    _____ x _____ = _____

7. How many claws?

    _____ x _____ = _____

# Answer Pages

**Page 3**
1. Answers will vary.   2. Thursday
3. 9                     4. 1
5. picture of clover     6. 7

**Page 4**

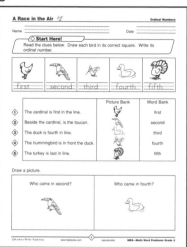

**Page 5**

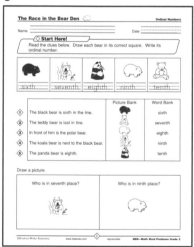

**Page 6**

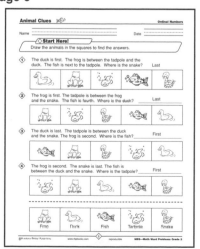

**Page 7**
1. Abbie
2. Brooke
3. nine
4. six

**Page 8**
1. 15 hippos
2. 16 monkeys
3. 16 kangaroos
4. 11 lions

**Page 9**
1. $5+9=14$ bees
2. $4+8=12$ snails
3. $6+9=15$ flies
4. $2+6+7=15$ ladybugs

**Page 10**
1. 8 deer flies
2. 6 beetles
3. 6 dragonflies
4. 7 cocoons

**Page 11**
1. $11+6=17$
2. $7+7=14$
3. $18-5=13$
4. $14-1=13$
5. $3+3+3+3=12$
6. $13-2=11$

**Page 12**
1. $2+2+2=6$
2. $3+3=6$
3. $1+1+1+1+1+1=6$
4. $6+6=12$

**Page 13**
1. $2+2=4$
2. $6+6+6=18$
3. $4+4+4=12$
4. $6+8+4=18$
5. $2+2=4$, $8+8=16$, spiders
6. 0

**Page 14**
(Answers may vary.)
toucan, turkey, quail, eagle
owl, hummingbird, penguin, woodpecker
eagle, woodpecker, penguin, hummingbird
crow, owl, toucan, turkey

**Page 15**
(Answers may vary.)
1. down, left, left, down
2. right, down, down
3. right, right, right, up, up
4. down, down, right, right, right

**Page 16**
1. 40°F, 10°F, 90°F, 20°F, 70°F
2. cold, cold, warm, cold, warm
3. 90°F 44°F
4. 60°F 20°F

**Page 17**

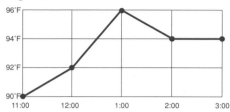

1. 92°F
2. 1:00
3. 2:00
4. 12:00

**Page 18**
1. monkey
2. bear
3. squirrel
4. elephant
5. lizard

**Page 19**
1. monkey
2. elephant
3. 20 pounds
4. elephant
5. 8 pounds

**Page 20**
1. 21
2. 2
3. monkeys
4. hippos
5. lions
6. 4
7. monkey

**Page 21**
1. 30
2. hummingbird
3. sea gull
4. 100
5. 60
6. 50, 60, 70, 90, 100, 120
7. 120, 100, 90, 70, 60, 50

**Page 22**
1–4. Answers will vary.

**Page 23**
1. Answers will vary.
2. koala
3. tiger
4. Answers will vary.

# Answer Pages

**Page 24**
1. 7, 10-3=7
2. 12, 7+5=12
3. 12-2=10
4. 14, 10+4=14

**Page 25**
1. 15
2. 40
3. 50
4. 20
5. 30
6. Answers will vary.

**Page 26**
1. 17+19=36
2. bears, 16+16=32 > 14+15=29
3. 16+14=30
4. Answers will vary.

**Page 27**
1. yes
2. no
3. yes

**Page 28**
1. 20
2. 21
3. 14
4. 11
5. 13
6. Answers will vary.

**Page 29**
1. 25+25+25=75
2. 22+22+22=66
3. 15+15=30
4. 4+4+4+4=16

**Page 30**
1. 5x2=10
2. 6x1=6
3. 5x2=10
4. 4x4=16
5. 5x2=10
6. 3x4=12
7. 4x2=8

# Rainbow Bridge Publishing
# Certificate
# of Completion

Awarded to

_____

for the completion of

## Mastering Basic Skills

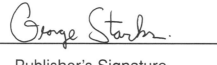
_____

Publisher's Signature

_____

Parent's Signature

---

# Receive RBP's FREE Parent and Teacher on-line newsletter!

Receive special offers, FREE learning exercises and great ideas to use in your classroom and at home!

**To receive our on-line newsletter, please provide us with the following information:**

Name:_____

Address:_____

City:_____ State: ____ Zip: _____

Email Address:_____

Store where book was purchased: _____

Child's grade level: _____

Book title purchased:_____

**Or visit our website:**

## www.sbakids.com

**Or Call:**
**801-268-8887**

## Summer Bridge Activities™

| Title | Price |
| --- | --- |
| Grade P-K | $12.95 |
| Grade K-1 | $12.95 |
| Grade 1-2 | $12.95 |
| Grade 2-3 | $12.95 |
| Grade 3-4 | $12.95 |
| Grade 4-5 | $12.95 |
| Grade 5-6 | $12.95 |

## Summer Bridge Middle School™

| Title | Price |
| --- | --- |
| Grade 6-7 | $12.95 |
| Grade 7-8 | $12.95 |

## Summer Bridge Reading Activities™

| Title | Price |
| --- | --- |
| Grade 1-2 | $6.95 |
| Grade 2-3 | $6.95 |
| Grade 3-4 | $6.95 |

## Summer Journal™

| Title | Price |
| --- | --- |
| Summer Journal™ | $4.95 |

## Summer Dailies™

| Title | Price |
| --- | --- |
| Summer Dailies™ | $4.95 |

## Summer Traveler™

| Title | Price |
| --- | --- |
| Summer Traveler™ | $4.95 |

## Math Bridge™

| Title | Price |
| --- | --- |
| Grade 1 | $9.95 |
| Grade 2 | $9.95 |
| Grade 3 | $9.95 |
| Grade 4 | $9.95 |
| Grade 5 | $9.95 |
| Grade 6 | $9.95 |
| Grade 7 | $9.95 |
| Grade 8 | $9.95 |

## Reading Bridge™

| Title | Price |
| --- | --- |
| Grade 1 | $9.95 |
| Grade 2 | $9.95 |
| Grade 3 | $9.95 |
| Grade 4 | $9.95 |
| Grade 5 | $9.95 |
| Grade 6 | $9.95 |
| Grade 7 | $9.95 |
| Grade 8 | $9.95 |

## Skill Builders™

| Title | Price |
| --- | --- |
| Phonics Grade 1 | $2.50 |
| Spelling Grade 2 | $2.50 |
| Vocabulary Grade 3 | $2.50 |
| Reading Grade 1 | $2.50 |
| Reading Grade 2 | $2.50 |
| Reading Grade 3 | $2.50 |
| Math Grade 1 | $2.50 |
| Math Grade 2 | $2.50 |
| Math Grade 3 | $2.50 |
| Subtraction Grade 1 | $2.50 |
| Subtraction Grade 2 | $2.50 |
| Multiplication Grade 3 | $2.50 |

## Connection Series™

| Title | Price |
| --- | --- |
| Reading Grade 1 | $10.95 |
| Reading Grade 2 | $10.95 |
| Reading Grade 3 | $10.95 |
| Math Grade 1 | $10.95 |
| Math Grade 2 | $10.95 |
| Math Grade 3 | $10.95 |

## Mastering Basic Skills™

| Title | Price |
| --- | --- |
| Grammar Grade 1 | $5.95 |
| Grammar Grade 2 | $5.95 |
| Grammar Grade 3 | $5.95 |
| Word Problems Grade 1 | $4.95 |
| Word Problems Grade 2 | $4.95 |
| Word Problems Grade 3 | $4.95 |
| Word Problems Grade 4 | $4.95 |
| Listening Skills Grade 1 | $4.95 |
| Listening Skills Grade 2 | $4.95 |
| Listening Skills Grade 3 | $4.95 |

## Math Test Preparation™

| Title | Price |
| --- | --- |
| Math Test Prep Grade 1 | $10.95 |
| Math Test Prep Grade 2 | $10.95 |
| Math Test Prep Grade 3 | $10.95 |

## First Step Spanish™

| Title | Price |
| --- | --- |
| Colors/Shapes | $5.95 |
| Alphabet/Numbers | $5.95 |

**Available everywhere!
Visit your favorite bookstore.**

Place
Proper
Postage
Here

**Rainbow Bridge Publishing
PO Box 571470
Salt Lake City, Utah 84157**

Keeping Children Busy, Happy, and Learning During the Summer and Beyond!